Mark Fullerton

D0191860

The End of Christendom

by
Malcolm Muggeridge

Introduction by
JOHN NORTH

Grand Rapids
WILLIAM B. EERDMANS PUBLISHING COMPANY

Copyright © 1980
by Wm. B. Eerdmans Publishing Company
255 Jefferson Ave. S.E., Grand Rapids, Mich. 49503
All rights reserved
Printed in the United States of America

Library of Congress Cataloging in Publication Data

Muggeridge, Malcolm, 1903-
The end of Christendom.

Based on the author's Pascal lecture series given
in 1978 at the University of Waterloo, Ontario.
1. Christianity—Essence, genius, nature—
Addresses, essays, lectures. 2. Church history—
Addresses, essays, lectures. 1. Title.
BT60.M83   270   80-11993
ISBN 0-8028-1837-4 (pbk.)

Contents

Introduction

*Man is obviously made for thinking. Therein lies all his
dignity and his merit; and his whole duty is to think as
he ought. Now the order of thought is to begin with
ourselves, and with our author and our end.*

Blaise Pascal, Pensée 620

*We know the truth not only through our reason but also
through our heart. It is through the latter that we know
first principles, and reason, which has nothing to do
with it, tries in vain to refute them.*

Pensée 110

*It is quite certain that there is no good without the
knowledge of God; that the closer one comes, the hap-
pier one is, and the further away one goes, the more
unhappy one is, and that ultimate unhappiness would
be to be certain of the opposite [to him].*

Pensée 432

The two essays in this volume are the text of the
inaugural addresses of The Pascal Lectures on Christianity and the University, given at the University
of Waterloo by Malcolm Muggeridge in October,
1978. Blaise Pascal (1632-1662) is remembered today

as the forerunner of Newton in the establishment of calculus, and as the author of his Christian meditations, *Les Pensées.* Members of the University of Waterloo, wishing to commemorate the spirit of Pascal, have established this annual lecture series to generate discourse within the university community on some aspect of its own world, its theories, its research, its leadership role in our society, challenging the university to a search for truth through personal faith and intellectual inquiry which focus on Jesus Christ.

Most of the great universities of the West were founded with the conviction that theology is the queen of the disciplines, and that the key to man's wholeness is the pursuit of the truth of God through Jesus Christ. Apart from that truth, it was believed, all other expressions of truth are fragmentary and sterile. Now, in the latter part of the twentieth century, that tradition has almost disappeared. Where Jesus Christ and Christian doctrine are the subject of formal study, it is usually as a minor area of Comparative Religion or in a divinity school well segregated from the general student body. Religious enthusiasm among students is an embarrassment; belief in the authority of the Bible and the deity of Jesus Christ is treated as naivety to be enlightened rather than life to be nourished. Scholars in the arts, letters, and sciences who show signs of Christian devotion are likely to be shrugged off as simplistic and eccentric. Coincidentally, truth itself has become devalued, especially in the humanities and social sciences and increasingly in the pure sciences, its consequence and even existence a matter of doubt. Universities seem to promote fragmentation, in part by undermining general studies in favor of specialized and practical studies, in part by ignoring the signs of decay in the spiritual, moral, and emotional health of the academic community. In this context the pertinence of the spirit of Blaise Pascal is evident.

Pascal is remarkable for the wholeness of his vision. The seventeenth century in France was the golden age of modern science, and also a century of great religious revival. So when the young Blaise began to look beyond mathematics and science in his restless search for more encompassing truths, he found a large, active community of scholars in philosophy, metaphysics, and religion. The fruitfulness of his explorations and of his Christian conversion is evident in the profound insights of *Les Pensées,* but goes further insofar as he was able to develop a unified, integrated understanding of human experience. Committing himself to the glorification of Jesus Christ throughout the remainder of his life, Pascal did not leave behind his mathematics and science. He discovered that thoroughgoing rationality is consistent with ardent worship of the living God, that one can love God with his mind and use his mind in the service of God. Albert N. Wells points out in his introductory volume, *Pascal's Recovery of Man's Wholeness* that in finding Jesus Christ to be the single ground of all truth, Pascal was being consistent with the principle of thought behind all his work. That is, behind all complexity and fragmentation lies a simple, unifying truth to be discovered. For example, his development of the calculating machine utilized a single idea, the mechanical counting of turns of a wheel, to perform all the basic operations of arithmetic. The idea is so rich that it has been used to govern the operation of our speedometers, tachometers, and electronic computers. Again, in the geometry of conic projections he proposed a single theorem which gave rise to over four hundred propositions covering the entire field. Similarly, in religion he discovered what many have accepted but fewer have explored to the same extent: that in Jesus Christ is the coherence of all human experience, a source of satisfaction for the mind to which even mathematics points, but also for the spirit and personality. He concluded:

> Reason's last step is the recognition that there are an infinite number of things which are beyond it. It is merely feeble if it does not go as far as to realize that.

Pensée 188

Natural theology and rationalistic philosophy were, apart from the faith in God which is the condition of true rationality, only "proud reasonings" attempting to order reality according to the laws of the mind. Because selfhood is prior to rationality, because man is far more than he knows about himself or his world, intellectual wholeness depends upon ethical, spiritual wholeness; all depend upon man's experience of the reality of Christ:

> It is good to be tired and wearied by the vain search after the true good, that we may stretch out our arms to the Redeemer.... We only know God by Jesus Christ. Without this mediator all communion with God is taken away; through Jesus Christ we know God.... Jesus Christ is then the true God of men.
>
> Pensées 422, 546

Although he continued his work in science, mathematics, and metaphysics, he did not confuse matters of faith with matters of reason, nor produce a religious scientism which by attempting to force a reconciliation between religion and science would have threatened the integrity of both. Finally, he did not lose himself in mysticism at the expense of the community—his omnibus system which became the basis of public transport in Paris was developed in the latter part of his life.

Malcolm Muggeridge is a fitting choice to inaugurate the Pascal Lectures on Christianity and the University. During the first half of the twentieth century, he moved easily among the renowned: politicians, scientists, academics, churchmen, and socialites. As a commentator in the press, then radio and television, he became increasingly caustic about

the figures and movements of our time. Disillusion-
ment mounting at times to anger began to charac-
terize his work. Then came a transformation as
wholehearted as that of Pascal, and in allegiance to
the same master. The focus of his work has changed
from the superstars to the meek of the earth: to the
mentally disabled in the care of John Vanier at
L'Arche, in Oise province, France; or to the quietly
industrious women working with Mother Theresa in
Calcutta. He has also drawn our attention again to
the disdained artists: the mad William Blake, the
epileptic Fyodor Dostoevsky, the imprisoned and ex-
iled Solzhenitsyn. In each he has detected the work
of Jesus Christ, an influence promoting wholeness in
the midst of their personal tragedies. He reminds us
that in our own search for wholeness we have such
testimonies as these for our consideration.

As Muggeridge's tone has changed from the satiric
to the prophetic, he has received the indignation
accorded every prophet. The forcefulness of his statements has been dismissed by some as exaggeration,
unbalance approaching monomania, or even personal bitterness. When in 1973 he resigned as Rector
of the University of Edinburgh rather than approve
the students' request for liberal distribution of "pot
and pills," ironically the two loudest voices denounc-
ing him were those of chaplains. He had complained
that the students on whom society lavished its resources in the expectation that they would spearhead
progress, producing great works of art, perception,

and understanding, were degrading themselves with "the resort of any old, slobbering debauchee anywhere in the world at any time— Dope and Bed." He said in his resignation address that the essential quest of the university and the highest aspiration of man is to see God; that to see God is to find understanding, to know the mystery of things, and cannot be achieved by the most perceptive and enlightened thinking, let alone by indulging the senses or doing good deeds, but by purity of heart. So he urged students to turn from the faddish art and literature of the university world—that of Pinter, Beckett, Burroughs, and the Beatles—as from the bad dreams of a materialistic world. So far as he was concerned, he said, it was Christ or nothing. Yet not a single public statement was made in support of Muggeridge's position.

The astringency of Muggeridge's comment when he is in a recording studio or on a public platform is in marked contrast with the gentleness of his personal life. He has a patience with every serious questioner, a quickness to tears over griefs of others which speaks of an imaginative range unknown to the rest of us. Each year his spirit seems brighter, his humor lighter. This meekness is far from paradoxical. Rather, as in Jesus himself, the clarity and power of the public voice is in large part explained by such handsomeness of heart.

John S. North
University of Waterloo

The End of Christendom

LADIES AND GENTLEMEN: Let me say at once that there is no sponsorship of a lecture which could appeal to me more than that of Pascal. Blaise Pascal is to me an infinitely sympathetic character. There is only one blot on his record, and that is that he invented the computer. That, I think, was a dastardly act, for which I am sure he has suffered a great deal in his contact with the higher authorities since he passed on. It is the only blot on an otherwise impeccable life.

I first picked up *Les Pensées* by chance some decades ago and found myself at once entranced by them. I hope very much that you may feel inclined to explore them yourselves—if possible in French, which would be the first serious and valuable dividend you would get from the Canadian government's bilingual policy. The thing which will strike you about Pascal, and in French even more than in translation, is the extraordinary skill and beauty of his language, the luminosity of his words, as he attempts the task of producing an apologia for the Christian faith. I have always had a sort of mania about words—it's the only consistent and abiding passion I have ever had. For that reason if for no other, Pascal made an immediate appeal. I think the most wonderful sentence ever penned is in the first chapter of St. John's Gospel, "In the beginning was the Word . . .". What a marvellous sentence that is. How tremendous are its implications. "In the beginning was the Word. . . ." It had to be the Word. It couldn't be, for instance, "In the beginning was video tape . . .", "In the beginning was celluloid . . .", or "In the beginning was a microphone . . ."—none of that. In the beginning was the Word, and one of the things that appalls me and saddens me about the world today is the condition of words. Words can be polluted even more dramatically and drastically than rivers and land and sea. There has been a terrible destruction of words in our time.

Let me give a striking example. Perhaps the most beautiful of words, the subject of that marvellous thirteenth chapter of the Epistle to the Corinthians, is the word "love." Just think of how that word has been polluted and corrupted so that one scarcely dares to use it. Similarly with words like "freedom" and "liberation." The truth is that if we lose the meaning of words, it is far more serious in practise than losing our wealth or our power. Without our words, we are helpless and defenceless; their misuse is our undoing. For instance, we speak of liberalizing our abortion laws, which means simply facilitating more abortion. Or we speak of reforming our marriage laws, when we mean creating facilities for breaking more and more marriages. Jesus himself said that heaven and earth would pass away, but his words would not pass away. I believe that is true, and I think that our more sacred treasure today is the word of the Gospels, which we should guard at all costs, for it is most precious. Now Pascal is a master of words.

I was in Darwin, Australia, and I got a message that there was a man in a hospital there who had listened to something that I had said on the radio, and had expressed a wish that I should visit him. So I did. He turned out to be an old, wizened man who had lived in the bush and who was blind. I can never forget him. Wanting to think of something to say to him that would light him up and cheer him up, I suddenly remembered a phrase in the play *King Lear*. You may remember that Gloucester, commiserating with Lear on being blind, uses five words. I remembered them then: "I stumbled when I saw."[1] I said this to the old man in the Darwin hospital. He was utterly enchanted. He got the point immediately. As I left the ward, I could hear him saying them over and over to himself: "I stumbled when I saw." That is what I mean by the marvellous power of words when they are used with true force in their true meaning. You will find in the writings of Pascal this

[1] *King Lear*, IV.i.19.

very luminosity of words that is so precious.

When he died a young man, before he was forty, he had embarked on his great apologia for the Christian faith. His sister, Gilberte, who wrote a memoir of him, regretted that her brother had been unable to fulfill his dream in writing this apologia. All she had been able to find was some scribbled notes, which are what constitute *Les Pensées*. But it is quite likely that had Pascal lived to translate those notes into a long, well-reasoned thesis, it might have had infinitely less effect than they have had as *pensées*, which so touch people, so enchant you, as you read them because of their brevity, their sharpness, their rather haphazard quality. So again we have to say, "God moves in a mysterious way."

Next to this genius of Pascal's words I would draw your attention to the beautiful lucidity of his mind, the wonderful clarity of his thought. Like all true believers, he was deeply skeptical. His intelligence was wonderfully astringent and critical. It is one of the fantasies of the twentieth century that believers are credulous people, sentimental people, and that you have to be a materialist and a scientist and a humanist to have a skeptical mind. But of course exactly the opposite is true. It is believers who can be astringent and skeptical, whereas people who believe seriously that this universe exists only in order to provide a theatre for man must take man with deadly seriousness. I believe myself that the age we are living in now will go down in history as one of the most credulous ever. How could anyone look at television advertisements without reaching that conclusion? All those extraordinary potions that are offered to make your face beautiful, those things you can swallow to make your breath fragrant, are all apparently believed in to the extent that people buy the products. I have often thought that if I were a rich and adventurous man instead of an old and rather broken down one I should bring over a witch doctor from Africa and subject him to a course of television advertising and see how he would react. I think he would be green with envy. To think of all that weary slogging from African village to African village to dispose of his love potions and his jujus, while here, in the Western world, the most highly educated, the most progressive, the most advanced part of the earth, there is a reservoir of credulity beyond his wildest dreams. The truth is that the farther our faith reaches, the more doubts it encompasses, as from the highest hills there are the fullest vistas. Six lines of John Donne express this very beautifully. He refers to truth as on a mountain top, a craggy mountain top:

> Doubt wisely, in strange way
> To stand inquiring right is not to stray;
> To sleep, or run wrong, is. On a huge hill,
> Craggy and steep, Truth stands, and he that will
> Reach her, about must and about must go;
> And what the hill's suddenness resists, win so.[2]

[2]John Donne, "Satire III," 11. 78-83.

So you find in Pascal this wonderful astringency which seems a somewhat rare thing in a materialist age like ours.

Pascal was perhaps the most learned man of his time. Yet he put aside learning as a cul-de-sac and turned to faith. I was thinking, as I prepared these notes, that in old age faith seems to be the most marvellous possession anyone can have. People think of faith as being something that you don't really believe, a device in helping you believe simply it. Of course that is quite wrong. As Pascal says, faith is a gift of God. It is different from the proof of it. It is the kind of faith God himself places in the heart, of which the proof is often the instrument. Faith that makes us think of *credo* (I believe), rather than of *scio* (I know). He says of it, too, that it is the heart which is aware of God, and not reason. That is what faith is: God perceived intuitively by the heart, not by reason.

Faith does indeed tell us what the senses do not tell, but does not contradict their findings. It transcends but does not contradict them. Pascal repeats, "Faith is the gift of God." I think it is also the same thing that the poet William Blake, whom I so admire, calls the imagination. You know, we have got, as it were, mind blocks. So much has been achieved by human intelligence that we have got lost in it. Whereas this other dimension that Blake calls the imagination and that Pascal calls faith is the thing that we most desperately need. I am certain that in

—6—

eternity when we understand, and no longer see through a glass darkly but face to face, we shall find that all our efforts to convey the reality of our existence are just so much children's scribble in the light of what it really is. The scribbles that have come nearest to conveying it are those of the artists rather than those of the philosophers or the theologians or the scientists. Let me express that in one rather grotesque image. Imagine a savage abasing himself before a painted stone. Because that primitive act conveys faith of a kind, that savage is nearer to the realities of things than, say, Einstein. This is what Jesus meant with his sayings about how children and fools understand things that are hidden better than do the learned and the wise. We today need faith more than any other thing on the earth. In the writings of Pascal you will find faith expressed.

Pascal was also a very proud man. But he put aside his pride to bow himself down at the altar rail with his fellow Christians, whomsoever they might be, in perfect brotherliness. This was an important aspect of Pascal. Before scientists became as arrogant as many of them are today, he, a superlatively great scientist, practised true humility, which is the greatest of all virtues. Indeed, as he points out, humility is the very condition of virtue. Because he understood how important humility is and because he could recognize the arrogance that was growing up among scholars and learned people, he foresaw the dangers that the Enlightenment would bring. He knew that as never before in history a choice was going to confront man between seeing the whole future of mankind in terms of man shut up in his physical being—as we say today, in his genes—and the alternative of accepting in humility and contrition a role in the purposes of a loving God. Blaise Pascal is one of the choice spirits that I have encountered, one of the small, select company of those whose vision has enabled them to see life not just in the context of a particular time and particular historical situation but of eternity.

There is a special reason for welcoming Pascal as a sponsor of these lectures. He was the first and perhaps is still the most effective voice to be raised in warning of the consequences of the enthronement of the human ego in contradistinction to the cross, symbolizing the ego's immolation. How beautiful it all seemed at the time of the Enlightenment, that man triumphant would bring to pass that earthly paradise whose groves of academe would ensure the realization forever of peace, plenty, and beatitude in practice. But what a nightmare of wars, famines, and folly was to result therefrom.

On the title page of his copy of Bacon's *Advancement of Learning*, a key book in the coming of the age of science, Blake scribbled by way of comment, "Good advice for Satan's kingdom". And in his astoundingly prophetic novel *The Devils*, Dostoyevski makes his character Peter Vekovinsky, the liberal-anarchist figure sired by an authentic old liberal—as it might be, a male impersonator of Mrs. Eleanor Roosevelt—he makes Peter Vekovinsky say, "A generation or two of debauchery followed by a little sweet bloodletting, and the turmoil will begin." So indeed it has. No single novel is more worthwhile reading today than this astoundingly prophetic book, *The Devils*. Dostoyevski envisages in the context of nineteenth-century Russia precisely what we've seen, the story of our time. It is in fact the perfect artistic exposition of my theme, the downfall of Christendom, brought about by the death wish which necessarily accompanies the arrogance of the human mind.

These three people, Pascal, Blake, and Dostoyevski, illustrate perfectly what I have long believed to be the case, that history consists of parables whereby God communicates in terms that the imagination rather than the mind, faith rather than knowledge, can grasp. You know, there are many pleasures in being old and gaga. One of the greatest of them is to realize that history is largely nonsensical. How does this come about? Because when you get to be into your middle seventies, events and situations and circumstances that you very vividly and clearly remember are already history. Yet when you read them written as history they are completely and utterly unconvincing, with no possible resemblance to what you remember as the original on which they are based. So you have the pleasure of knowing that you need not bother in any way about history. The only reason for studying what goes on is to get at this parable that it conveys. Otherwise it is just like an interminable soap opera whose situations endlessly recur although the characters change.

As a matter of fact, it is not only of history that this is true. As John Henry Newman says, "Nature is a parable."[3] All creation, even our sins, everything that happens, all doing and considering, a leaf falling, a nuclear bomb exploding, the total experience of living, individually and collectively, carries God's messages as it were encoded. But we need the key to decipher them, to be able to decode them, and of course the key that came to us is the Incarnation. Through it we can get at what they have to say. It is on this basis that I approach my actual subject tonight, suggested to me by a chance remark, almost a throwaway line, by Archbishop Fulton Sheen. The line is that Christendom is over. Now that line thrown out by this distinguished prelate of the Roman Catholic Church held my attention. I want to approach the subject and see whether it is true, as I believe it to be.

People have been talking for a long time about the post-Christian era we are now living in. Al-

[3]John Henry Newman, *Apologia pro Vita Sua*. The reference is to his reading of Clement of Alexandria and Origen:

I understand these passages to mean that the exterior world, political and historical was but the manifestation to our senses of realities greater than itself. Nature was a parable; Scripture was an allegory, pagan literature, philosophy and mythology, properly understood, were but a preparation for the Gospel.

though the death of God has ceased to be a fashionable proposition, it is to the late rather than the living God that nowadays any reference to the deity is likely to be made. It's indicative, and I think highly significant, that it was Nietzsche who first announced God's demise. Then, growing bolder, he went on to insist that God had been murdered by his creature, man, this being, according to Nietzsche, the most glorious and promising event in human history. Not surprisingly, Nietzsche ended in an insane asylum in Venice and continued his observations about the death of God from a padded cell. But in a world that has itself gone mad like him, in excess of arrogance and self-conceit, his ravings continue to be seriously regarded, as for that matter do those of other lunatics down to and including the Marquis de Sade. Nietzsche dismissed Pascal contemptuously as a broken Christian.[4] As between the mad neo-pagan and the broken Christian, we may see in terms of a fearful symmetry the drama of our time.

"God is dead. Long live Superman," was Nietzsche's cry, and what supermen we've had, from Hitler to Muhammad Ali.[5] Whereas Pascal, in a wonderful passage, writes:

---

[4]Friedrich Wilhelm Nietzsche, *The Will To Power*, Book II, Part i, Section 252. *The Complete Works of Friedrich Nietzsche*, ed. Oscar Long (Edinburgh: T. N. Forelis, 1909), p. 207.

[5]Nietzsche, *Thus Spake Zarathustra*, Part I, Section 2. *Complete Works*, Volume 11, p. 6.

It is in vain oh men that you seek within yourselves the cure for your miseries. All your insight
only leads you to the knowledge that it is not in
yourselves that you will discover the true and the
good. The philosophers promised them to you and
they have not been able to keep their promise.
They do not know what your true good is or what
your true state is. How should they have provided
you with a cure for ills which they have not even
understood. Your principal maladies are pride,
which cuts you off from God, and sensuality, which
binds you to the earth. And they have done nothing but foster at least one of these maladies. If
they have given you God for your object, it has
been to pander to your pride. They have made
you think you were like him and resemble him by
your nature. And those who have grasped the van-
ity of such a pretension have cast you down in the
other abyss by making you believe that your nature
is like that of the beast of the field and have led
you to seek your good in lust, which is the lot of
animals.[6]

Two voices, Nietzsche's and Pascal's, about which the
world continues to hesitate.

God, of course, cannot die. He might not exist at
all, though I am more certain he does exist than I
am of my own existence. And indeed this has been
the conviction of all the greatest minds and most
creative spirits, as far as our Western civilization is

[6]Pascal, *Pensées*, 149.

concerned, at any rate, since Plato. By definition he belongs to eternity, not to time, and so is intrinsically immortal. The last Archbishop of Canterbury but one, Dr. Ramsey, appeared not to realize this when, to my amazement, at the end of a performance of *Godspell*, he rose to his feet and shouted: "Long live God," which, as I reflected at the time, was like shouting, "Carry on eternity" or "keep going infinity." The incident made a deep impression on my mind because it illustrated the basic difficulty I met with when I was editor of *Punch*: that the eminent so often say and do things which are infinitely more ridiculous than anything you can invent for them. That might not sound to you like a terrible difficulty but it is, believe me, the main headache of the editor of an ostensibly humorous paper. You go to great trouble to invent a ridiculous Archbishop of Canterbury and give him ridiculous lines to say and then suddenly he rises in his seat at the theatre and shouts out: "Long live God." And you're defeated, you're broken.

Christendom, however, is something quite different from Christianity, being the administrative or power structure, based on the Christian religion and constructed by men. It bears the same relation to the everlasting truth of the Christian revelation as, say, laws do to justice, or morality to goodness, or carnality to love—if you like, as Augustine's City of God to the earthly city where we temporarily live.

The founder of Christianity was, of course, Christ.

The End of Christendom

The founder of Christendom I suppose could be named as the Emperor Constantine. I believe and Bishop Sheen believes that it is not Christ's Christianity which is now floundering. You might even say that Christ himself abolished Christendom before it began by stating that his kingdom was not of this world—one of the most far reaching and important of all his statements. Christendom began with the Emperor Constantine. Christianity began with the Incarnation, that stupendous moment when, as it is put so marvellously in the Apocryphal book of Ecclesiasticus, "While all things were in quiet silence and the night was in the midst of her swift course, Thine Almighty Word leaped down from heaven, out of Thy royal throne. This Almighty Word is everlasting truth and so is valid forever."[7] Or, as I have already quoted our Lord himself, "Heaven and earth shall pass away, but my words shall not pass away."

Christendom, on the other hand, began when Constantine, as an act of policy, decided to tolerate, indeed positively favour, the Church, uniting it to the secular state by the closest possible ties. This was at the beginning of the fourth century. A parallel situation which might easily arise would be if the revival of Christianity in the U.S.S.R. reached a point at which the ruling oligarchy, the Communist Party, decided to absorb it into the state as an alternative ideology to Marxism, in the same sort of way

[7]The Wisdom of Solomon 18:14-15, from the Apocrypha.

that under the Czars the Russian Orthodox Church was absorbed into the state.

During the late '39-'45 war, in the darkest days of Russia when the German army was within a few miles of both Leningrad and Moscow, Stalin did a most extraordinary thing. You might have expected that as a convinced Marxist he would have had readings from *Das Kapital* on the Soviet radio in order to stiffen up the sinews and summon up the blood of his fellow countrymen. But he didn't do that, for the name of Marx was unmentioned in those dark days. What he did do was a characteristic Stalinist thing, he fetched the patriarch and one or two other prelates from the labour camp where they were languishing and brought them to the Kremlin and set them up in business again. In other words, he reestablished for the time being the Russian Orthodox Church. It's one of those very significant incidents that tends to get forgotten. I wonder what it must have been like in the camp when the poor old patriarch was told that Stalin wanted to set him up again. The order to get all his vestments and things would have come as quite a shock to him. But that is exactly what happened, because Stalin knew that to get the Russian people to fight to the end with their backs to the wall, he needed something more than Marxist materialism.

Now this easily might happen again. The people emerging as Christians in the U.S.S.R. may become so strong that the Soviet government will adopt Christianity. There's a large strain of irony in our

human affairs. Blake's phrase for it is "fearful symmetry." What a wonderful example of fearful symmetry it would be if on the selfsame day that Marxism
was thrown out of the Kremlin window the Vatican
was impelled by the pressure of Christian Marxist
dialogues with Jesuits and others to issue an encyc-
lical, *De Necessitate Marxisme*. Stranger things have
happened. This irony, we must be clear, is written
into our mortal existence. I love it. It's conveyed
beautifully in the medieval cathedrals, where you
have the steeple climbing up into the sky symbolizing
all the wonderful spiritual aspirations of human beings,
but at the same time, set in the same roof, you have
these little grinning gargoyles staring down at the
earth. The juxtaposition of these two things might
seem strange at first. But I contend that they are
aspects of the same essential attitude of mind, an
awareness that at the heart of our human existence
there is this mystery. Interwoven with our affairs is
this wonderful spirit of irony which prevents us from
ever being utterly and irretrievably serious, from being
unaware of the mysterious nature of our existence.

In any case, it's clear to me beyond any possibility
of doubt that Christendom has played a tremendous
role in the art and literature, in the mores and jur-
isprudence, in the architecture, values, institutions,
and whole way of life of Western man during the
centuries of his dominance in the world. But now as
Western man's power and influence recede, so Christendom itself comes to have an evermore ghostly air

about it, to the point that it seems to belong to history already, rather than to present-day actuality. It would be far beyond the scope of a single lecture, and indeed far beyond my capacity as a journalist rather than a scholar, to trace the course of the decline and fall of Christendom as Gibbon did that of the Roman Empire which preceded it. All I can do here is to indicate some of the contributory factors to its collapse.

First and foremost I should put a sort of death wish at the heart of it, in the guise of what we call liberalism. It goes back, as Solzhenitsyn suggested in his recent Harvard address,[8] to the Enlightenment and gained a great impetus during the period of American dominance in the world in this century, culturally and economically, if not militarily. Previous civilizations have been overthrown from without by the incursion of barbarian hordes. Christendom has dreamed up its own dissolution in the minds of its own intellectual elite. Our barbarians are home products, indoctrinated at the public expense, urged on by the media systematically stage by stage, dismantling Christendom, depreciating and deprecating all its values. The whole social structure is now tumbling down, dethroning its God, undermining all its certainties. All this, wonderfully enough, is being done in the name of the health, wealth, and happiness of

[8]Alexander Solzhenitsyn, *A World Split Apart:* Commencement Address delivered at Harvard University, June 8, 1978 (New York: Harper and Row, 1978), pp. 47-51.

all mankind. That is the basic scene that seems to me will strike a future Gibbon as being characteristic of the decline and fall of Christendom.

I could go on giving details, but you can very well fill in for yourselves: the internecine conflicts between the Western nations, the decline of Western power and influence, the collapse of the British Empire into which I was born. We used to boast that it was an empire on which the sun never set; now it's become a commonwealth in which the sun never rises. That's how far we've moved. I must also leave you to analyze the cultural decline of Western art and literature. In the cycle of a great civilization, the artist begins as a priest and ends as a clown or buffoon. Examples of buffoonery in twentieth-century art, literature, and music are many: Dali, Picasso, John Cage, Beckett.

Consider also our excessive, obsessive televiewing. The average Western man looks at television for four hours every day, which means that he spends ten years of his life looking into a television screen, something that precludes reading, conversation, and other exercises in literacy. About twenty years ago there was the twenty-fifth anniversary of the invention of television, a day that should have been signalized by wearing black and muffled bells and flags at half mast. However, the BBC decided in its wisdom to make a program showing men looking at television all over the world. Around the world this television crew went, filming people looking at television. It had no difficulty whatever finding them, in the deserts, on the tops of mountains, in the jungle—everywhere it went there was the little screen and people gathered round it. But what they discovered was that everybody was looking at the same programs: *I Love Lucy* and *Wagon Train*. So you had the ironic spectacle of the whole human race preoccupied with these great masterpieces of our civilization.

Another area of the moral and spiritual decline of Christendom is the abandonment of Christian mores. The movement away from Christian moral standards has not meant moving to an alternative humanistic system of moral standards as was anticipated, but moving into a moral vacuum, especially in the areas of eroticism. Christendom has also retreated from freedom. In the much talk today about human rights, we forget that our human rights are derived from the Christian faith. In Christian terms every single human being, whoever he or she may be, sick or well, clever or foolish, beautiful or ugly, every single human being is loved of his Creator, who has, as the Gospels tell us, counted the hairs of his head. This Creator cannot see even a sparrow fall to the ground without concern. Now it is from that concept that our rights derive. You will find as we move away from Christendom that whatever declarations may be made and agreements may be concluded, these basic human rights depend ultimately on the Christian concept of man and of his relationship to his Creator.

The West is also on a quest for security and plenty. The quest for security has given us a weapon so powerful that it can blow us and our earth to smithereens;

our quest for plenty has resulted in the exploitation of our resources to an unconscionable degree. So we come to thinking of the wrath to come. A dying civilization, Christendom, on a swiftly moving, ebbing tide, clutches at any novelty in art and literature, ready to accept and then almost at once reject whatever is new no matter how perverse or abnormal. We have "a weariness with striving to be men," as the American critic Leslie Fiedler put it,

> the more desolating because there's no God to turn to. God has been abolished by the media pundits and other promoters of our new demythologized divinity. We continue to insist that change is progress, self-indulgence is freedom and novelty is originality. In these circumstances it's difficult to avoid the conclusion that Western man has decided to abolish himself, creating his own boredom out of his own affluence, his own vulnerability out of his own strength, his own impotence out of his own erotomania, himself blowing the trumpet that brings the walls of his own city tumbling down. Having convinced himself that he is too numerous, he labours with pill and scalpel and syringe to make himself fewer, thereby delivering himself the sooner into the hands of his enemies. At last, having educated himself into imbecility and polluted and drugged himself into stupefaction, he keels over, a weary, battered old brontosaurus, and becomes extinct.[9]

You might think that was a somewhat pessimistic

[9]Leslie Fiedler, quoted in *Trousered Apes* by Duncan Williams.

way of looking at things, but it isn't really. I conclude that civilizations, like every other human creation, wax and wane. By the nature of the case there can never be a lasting civilization any more than there can be a lasting spring or lasting happiness in an individual life, or lasting stability in a society. It's in the nature of man and of all that he constructs to perish, and it must ever be so. The world is full of the debris of past civilizations, and others are known to have existed which have not even left any debris behind them but have just disappeared. This applies also to utopias of every kind, whatever their ideology may be, from the garden of Eden onwards. Such dreams of lasting felicity have cropped up and no doubt always will, but their realization is impossible for the simple reason that a fallen creature like man, though capable of conceiving perfection and aspiring after it, is in himself and in his works forever imperfect. Thus he's fated to exist in the no man's land between the perfection he can conceive and the imperfection that characterizes his own nature and everything he does. It is a tantalizing situation, and yet one that has produced whatever is truly great in the way of human achievements.

In these circumstances why should anyone expect Christendom to go on forever or see in its impending collapse a cosmic catastrophe? Our earth and its inhabitants have survived numerous disasters from the Ice Age onwards. We will doubtless likewise survive many others, including, if it happens, a breakdown of the present world order, whether in consequence of nuclear warfare or, less dramatically and perhaps more probably, of the breakdown of law and order and the degeneracy of a population grown soft by excessive self-indulgence and confused by the collapse of standards of belief and behaviour which have hitherto been acceptable to them even though only imperfectly observed. If, then, all the signs point to the decline and impending fall of what we continue to call Western Civilization, to be followed by another Dark Age, this no more represents any finality in human history than other such developments have in the past.

I think of St. Augustine when in A.D. 410 the news was brought to him in Carthage that Rome had been sacked. It was a sore blow, but as he explained to his flock, "All earthly cities are vulnerable. Men build them and men destroy them. At the same there is the City of God which men did not build and cannot destroy and which is everlasting." Then he devoted the remaining seventeen years of his life to an exposition of the relation between the two cities in his great masterpiece, *The City of God*, thereby providing a basis for coping with the collapse of a spent civilization, lighting a way through the darkness that followed into a new civilization, Christendom, whose legatees and perhaps liquidators we are. Said Blake: "I give you the end of a golden string, and you wind it into ball. It will lead you in at heaven's gate, built in Jerusalem's wall."[10] Let us then avert our eyes from the wrath to come, which

[10]William Blake, *Jerusalem*, ll. 1-4.

would seem now to be upon us, and like Augustine follow Blake's golden string beyond the impending darkness. For it is in the breakdown of power rather than in its triumph that men may discern its true nature and in an awareness of their own inadequacy when confronted with such a breakdown that they can best understand who and what they are.

Twentieth-century man has created his own fantasy through science which has enabled him to explore as no other generation of men have the structure and mechanics of his own environment. What fantastic achievements have thereby been made possible in the way of moving faster, growing richer, communicating more rapidly, mastering illnesses, and altogether overcoming the hazards of our earthly existence. But all the achievements have led to a growing arrogance, a widening separation from the true nature of our being; in other words, an alienation from God. If it were possible to live without God, it would not be worth living at all. It was in a labour camp, Solzhenitsyn has told us, that he learnt what freedom meant and became free. So, amidst the shambles of a fallen Christendom, I feel a renewed confidence in the light of the Christian revelation with which it first began. I should hate you to think that his view that I've put before you is a pessimistic view. Strangely enough I believe it to be the only way to a proper and real hope.

You know, it's a funny thing that when you're very old, as I am, seventy-five and near to dying, the queerest thing happens. You very often wake up about two or three in the morning and you are half in and half out of your body, a most peculiar situation. You can see your battered old carcass there between the sheets and it's quite a tossup whether you resume full occupancy and go through another day or make off where you can see, like the lights in the sky as you're driving along, the lights of Augustine's *City of God.* In that sort of limbo, between being in and out of your body, you have the most extraordinary confidence, a sharpened awareness that this earth of ours with all its inadequacies is an extraordinarily beautiful place, that the experience of living in it is a wonderful, unique experience, that relations with other human beings, human love, human procreation, work, all these things are marvellous and wonderful despite all that can be said about the difficulty of our circumstances; and finally, a conviction passing all belief that as a minute particle of God's creation, you are a participant in his purposes for his creation and that those purposes are loving and not malign, are creative and not destructive, are universal and not particular. In that confidence is an incredible comfort and an incredible joy.

QUESTION 1:

Mr. Muggeridge, you put down Nietzsche because he went insane after he wrote most of his works and yet you exalt Dostoyevski, but you leave out something. That is, Dos-

toyevski became an avid Christian before he became a writer, and as a result of being hauled in front of a firing squad for being a liberal, when just before he was going to be shot, the messenger for the Czar came in and said "You're saved. You're not going to be shot". Now imagine what this shock would do. It would either make a man a slave to the Czar or a raving lunatic and I say that he became both in becoming a Christian. At least Nietzsche lost his mind after he wrote his stuff but Dostoyevski before he wrote.

MUGGERIDGE:

That's a very ingenious idea. Actually it was the very beginning of his life that this episode took place, when he was in his early twenties. He wrote *The Devils* in middle age, so that I don't think it's quite on all fours with Nietzsche, who definitely was demented and whose dementia took the form of repeating all the stuff that he's written in his books. So I don't think the two cases are the same. Dostoyevski, it's true, was an epileptic, but I don't think you can hold that against him, although he himself thought his epilepsy was associated with his mental abilities. There's a remarkable account in another novel of his called *The Idiot*, of having an epileptic fit. An extraordinary illumination came to him before this fit seized him. But I don't think that Dostoyevski was ever mad in the sense that Nietzsche was. And Nietzsche's remarks about superman and all that mad egomania have had an enormous influence on the twentieth century.

Are there other questions?

QUESTION 2:

*Do you think Nietzsche was correct when he said that we
have murdered God?*

MUGGERIDGE:

He went further than that and said that we have
murdered him and this is the most glorious event in
human history. I would find it difficult to see in that
any kind of sense either that God was still alive and
that he regretted His passing. I'm not criticizing him
because I think he was mad. What I'm interested in
is that his madness should have had such an extraordinary effect on the twentieth century. The poor fellow in his loony bin in Venice is a subject for
compassion obviously. There's a very touching paint-
ing of him sitting at the window of this hospital and
saying goodbye to the sun. His madness coincided
with, in my opinion, a great deal of the madness of
the twentieth century, whereas in Pascal, whom he
called a broken Christian, I see very much the
opposite.

QUESTION 3:

*Mr. Muggeridge, what do you have to say to the established
Church in the West, which at this point has at least one
foot still in Christendom?*

MUGGERIDGE:

I think it depends entirely where you think the other foot is.

QUESTION 4:

Mr. Muggeridge, please elaborate on your statement that all believers are truly skeptical.

MUGGERIDGE:

The higher the hill that you climb, the bigger, the wider the vista that presents itself. The nearer you get to comprehending the true nature of our existence, the more possibility there is of being skeptical about our capacity to express that understanding. This is one of the points of those lines of John Donne which I quoted. Donne was himself a great Christian and writer of the most beautiful metaphysical verse. In climbing up to the top of this craggy mountain, you go round and round and round, and in going round, the doubting, or the wondering what the total conviction is, usually implies a very simple conviction. As you enter into what that wonderful fourteenth-century writer calls "the cloud of unknowing,"[11] as you become aware of that simple conviction, your doubts, your uncertainties are sharpened, not muffled. To believe greatly, it's necessary to doubt greatly.

[11]*A Book of Contemplation the which is called the Cloud of Unknowing in the which a soul is oned with God.* Edited from the British Museum MS. Harl 674 with an introduction by Evelyn Underhill (London: J. M. Watkin, 1912). The author is an anonymous fourteenth-century mystic.

You know, humour is an expression of skepticism, of this disparity between what we aspire after and what we achieve. The greatest humourists, like Cervantes and Rabelais and Gogol and Shakespeare too, have all been believers, contrary to what is often supposed, whereas materialists are very serious people indeed because if you believe only in man, then you must hold man in great veneration.

QUESTION 5:

At what point in your life did you believe in Christ Jesus?

MUGGERIDGE:

It's a question I often get asked, but I can't answer it. For me there has never been a moment when I would say at that point I believed. It's been much more like the journey of Bunyan's Pilgrim.

QUESTION 6:

What made you so skeptical?

MUGGERIDGE:

I've always been a skeptic. I instinctively disbelieve almost everything but because I disbelieve much I find it possible to believe. I agree that sounds slightly paradoxical. Now I mean that in utter seriousness because I can tell from the way you're asking that you understand. It does sound like a paradox but it's not. We know that we can't know. We know that whatever we manage to convey of the eternal mysteries of life is the most rudimentary sort of scribble.

The further we go in grasping the dimension of those eternal truths, the more skeptical we must be about our efforts to convey it. That's what I was getting at. As for myself, I can't say, it would be impossible for me to say, that at that point I believed or that at that point I disbelieved. I just struggled along feeling from the beginning convinced of one thing, which I think perhaps is the basic nature of a religious faith, that in this world I am a stranger. I don't belong here. I am staying here for a bit and it's a very nice place, an interesting place, but I don't belong here. From the beginning I can remember that feeling and I have it still.

QUESTION 7:

Mr. Muggeridge, when Nietzsche and other modern atheistic philosophers announce to us the death of God, are they not saying that God is not a part of our world? And is this not true from a Christian standpoint? God is not like a tree or another person. He infinitely transcends our world and is infinitely at the heart of it?

MUGGERIDGE:

I don't think that's true. The point of the Incarnation is that God became a man in order that He should be besides the immanent God, part of our human scene. That's why the Incarnation was such an extraordinary event, why it has had such a dramatic effect on human history.

QUESTION 8:

How can Christianity bring its insights to bear on the structure of the state?

MUGGERIDGE:

If I am correct that Christendom is over but Christ is not over, that the influence of Christ is not over (and there is evidence of an astonishing survival not of the Russian Orthodox Church but of Christ in the U.S.S.R.), then in that survival lies the promise of freedom again. But of course the Western world can very well lose freedom, at any rate temporarily. There can be another Dark Age.

QUESTION 9:

In your book Jesus Rediscovered *I believe you said why you were not a member at that time of the official church in England. Has that position of yours changed?*

MUGGERDIGE:

No, it has not changed. I do feel the same about the Church of England. I think it's probably a weakness in me that it should be so, but that's how I feel. It would be dishonest to suggest otherwise.

QUESTION 10:

What do you feel is the responsibility of the Christian towards the visible church which partakes both of this spiritual nature and of the institutional nature?

MUGGERIDGE:

It has to be left to the individual Christian to decide. I don't think anybody would presume—certainly I wouldn't—to lay down the rules about it.

QUESTION 11:

Mr. Muggeridge, I have heard your Third Testament on television and I was wondering why you chose not to include Albert Schweitzer in the series.

MUGGERIDGE:

I did think of him as a possible subject in that series. The heroic life of Albert Schweitzer is beyond any question, but I could not have used that particular life in the series with conviction. I wanted to do John Henry Newman, as a matter of fact, as one of the *Third Testament* figures. But I would have found difficulty in doing Schweitzer partly because his quest for the historical Jesus[12] was not a book that I found wholly sympathetic, since I'm not really interested in the historical Jesus side. I'm interested in a completely different attitude of mind, not in the fact that he related his Christianity so entirely to works. There is not in his writings the particular quality of mysticism that I was looking for. But I think he was a very remarkable man of our time.

[12]Albert Schweitzer, *The Quest of the Historical Jesus* (London: Black, 1910), translated by W. Montgomery. Published originally in German, at Tübingen, 1906.

QUESTION 12:

You commented about the Russian Orthodox Church and the way it allied itself with the Czar in order to maintain itself. I wonder if you see a parallel between that and the phenomenon we see happening in America of the novelty of being born again, of a close association between an American religion and the American way, a religion that bolsters the American way. How do you view that trend?

MUGGERIDGE:

You could say the same thing about the established Church in England. The Anglican Church is part of the structure of the State, and its archbishops and bishops are appointed by the government, not by the Church. Wherever you get that you have a great weakening of the spiritual position. In the present situation of the overt Russian Orthodox Church in the U.S.S.R., which has the bishops and patriarchs and metropolitans, the leadership has to make terrific concessions to the Soviet government. On the other hand, through making those concessions, certain churches in Moscow and Leningrad and Kiev remain open. Beautiful services are made available, the very beautiful words of the Gospels are read aloud. In these matters you have to weigh the relative advantages and disadvantages. You can't take a definitive position about it. The solace of those services is so great, the importance of those words being kept alive and in circulation is so important, that the sacrifices, the compromises that are made must be accepted. But

it's a very difficult equation to work out. It's the
equation with which our Lord himself left us, that
we must render unto God the things that are God's
and unto Caesar the things that are Caesar's. He
neglected to tell us what proportion we owed, so that
of course people like myself can hope to get by with
offering Caesar very little. But the decision has to be
made as between the two.

QUESTION 13:

*If Christ is still alive, in what do you see his contemporary
expression as incarnation?*

MUGGERIDGE:

One example is the renewal of Christian faith in the
U.S.S.R. and, in a different way, in the satellite
countries, against all the odds. The strange and mysterious and highly amusing thing is that probably you
would have very great difficulty in finding a single
Marxist in the U.S.S.R. You would only find Marx-
ists among left-wing Jesuits in the faculties of universities in the West, which is one of God's little
jokes. It is possible that the bosses of the Russian
regime will decide that they want to get rid of Marxism. I think that in the U.S.S.R. everybody is heart-
ily sick of it. Nobody can read Marxist books because
they're so tedious. Therefore the question of agreeing
with them or not doesn't arise. But even then they're
sick of it, I think. So as this unexpected tide of Christian faith develops, the temptation to grab it will be

very great. To do so would also be a help in dealing
with the satellites like Poland and Hungary. It would
be extraordinarily funny. You see I've always thought
that the Cold War when it was on was one of the
most bizarre wars in history because wherever you
had the Americans, they created Communists and
wherever you had the Communists they created anti-
Communists. So that really the Cold War became
the question of whether the Americans would create
more Communists than the Russians would create
anti-Communists. At the present moment the Americans are doing rather well.

But Not of Christ

The first half of my subject has been "The End of Christendom." Now I come to the more attractive subject but also the more difficult one, "But Not of Christ." How, I want to ask myself and you, in the shambles of a collapsed Christendom, stands Christ? It's not all that easy to simplify this question, because in the strange maelstrom of today so many different Christs are being presented to us: Christ the guerrilla fighter; Christ the honourable member for Galilee South—Christ in all sorts of roles. The Sermon on the Mount becomes the Sermon on the Barricades in many people's estimation. Yet, I know and you know that there is still Christ, the figure who was the centre of the whole drama of the Incarnation, whom—if we look hard enough and have a pure heart—we can find.

I say, "How stands Christ?" a question that the apostle Paul might well have put with reference to a collapsing Roman empire. Remember that the emperor in charge at the time of the apostle Paul's evangelistic journeys was none other than Nero, a ruler who makes even ours seem positively sensible and restrained. Yet, I believe the question would scarcely have occurred to Paul, since the Christ he preached as the light of the world, as the crucified Saviour of the world, had nothing to do with the future destinies or past glories of the Roman or any other empire. Of course, the early Christians had the great advantage of believing that the world would soon come to an end. That was a sort of miracle in their favour because it prevented them occupying their minds with irrelevant matters. Dr. Johnson said that the prospect of being hanged wonderfully concentrates the mind. So does the prospect of the end of the world. It would have been difficult for the early Christians to worry their heads about, say, nationalizing the trams in Corinth, given their expectation quite a short time afterwards the whole show would come to an end. So it was in many ways advantageous.

In Paul's eyes, the Incarnate Presence, Jesus, was the centre of everything. It was in him that all Paul's evangelizing was centred, and Paul's preaching was in that sense wonderfully simple. Of course, in his incarnate presence Jesus was in fact the centre of everything. But in human terms, Jesus was an insignificant enough individual belonging to a subject people in one of the remoter dependencies of imperial Rome, whose brief ministry as recounted in the Gospels contained only a single, noncommittal, but exceedingly shrewd reference to the occupying power and its fiscal demands. You remember his famous reply, which has echoed through the centuries, when he was asked as a quick question whether tribute should be paid to Caesar. His answer was that we should "render unto Caesar the things that are Caesar's, and unto God the things that are God's."[1] The cleverness of that reply was of course that it didn't specify exactly how much was due to Caesar and how much to God. He left us to work that out, and it's possible, as I have discovered in the course of my long life, to whittle down what's due to Caesar in favour of what's due to God.

As for the decadent practices of Roman citizens such as the Corinthians—a general immorality so very reminiscent of today—these, Paul insisted, pertained to the dying world of paganism. Christians who had been reborn into the kingdom proclaimed by Christ, a kingdom whose fulfillment they awaited with confidence, were not to contaminate themselves with the moral squalor of the pagan world. Now we see Christendom likewise sinking. But the true point I want to make is this: that Christ's kingdom remains. Indeed, it can be seen more clearly and appreciated more sharply by contrast with the darkness and depravity of the contemporary scene.

Some might doubt the validity of such a proposition, confused as they are by contrary persuasion from the media, as well sometimes as from ostensible

[1]Mark 12:17.

spokesmen for the various Christian churches. For such spokesmen, the dismantling and distortion of the Christian faith and worship signifies that his kingdom is of this world: that treasure must be laid up on earth in the shape of an ever expanding gross national product; that the flesh lusts *with* (not against) the spirit and the spirit *with* (not against) the flesh, so that we have an obligation to do whatever we have a mind to. To those who might be troubled or disturbed by such distortions, a wonderful sign has been vouchsafed us, one of the great miracles of the story of Christendom. This sign is the amazing renewal of the Christian faith in its purest possible form in, of all places, the countries that have been most drastically subjected to the oppression and brainwashing and general influence of the first overtly atheistic and materialistic regime to exist on earth. This is a fact. I should say myself that it is the most extraordinary single fact of the twentieth century.

True, this fact receives only very scanty attention in the media. A strange thing I have observed over many years in this business of news gathering and news presentation is that by some infallible process media people always manage to miss the most important thing. It's almost as though there were some built-in propensity to do this. In moments of humility, I realize that if I had been correspondent in the Holy Land at the time of our Lord's ministry, I should almost certainly have spent my time knocking about with the entourage of Pontius Pilate, finding out what the Sanhedrin was up to, and lurking around Herod's court with the hope of signing up Salome to write her memoirs exclusively. I regret that this is true. Ironically enough, as the dramatization of the public scene gains impetus, so we move farther and farther from the reality of things and become more and more preoccupied with fantasy.

If when I was a young correspondent in Moscow in the early thirties you had said to me that it would be possible for the Soviet regime to continue for sixty years with its policy of doing everything possible to extirpate the Christian faith, to discredit its record and its originator, and that after this there would emerge figures like Solzhenitsyn speaking the authentic language of the Christian, grasping such great Christian truths as the cross in a way that few people do in our time, I would have said "No, it's impossible, it can't be." But I would have been wrong.

I once had occasion to conduct an interview with a Soviet writer. He was not a particularly well known but a relatively successful writer who had sought asylum in the United Kingdom, so I spent two or three days with him soon after his arrival. His name was Anatoli Kusnyetsov.[2] We discussed this ironic turn

---

[2]Anatoli Kusnyetsov, 1929-. An editor of the Gorkii Institute of Literature, Moscow, and winner of several literary competitions, Kusnyetsov settled in the United Kingdom in 1969. Among his published works are *Sequel of a Legend* (1957), *At Home* (1964), *Babi Yar* (1966), *Fire* (1969), and several film scenarios.

of events in his country. I noticed to my unutterable surprise that in his explanation of his conduct, of how his mind had developed, and of how he saw the world, the influence of the Christian faith was very marked. I asked him point-blank how this could be. After all, Soviet citizens had no access to the Gospels, few religious services available (at that time fewer than now), no literature of the mystics, no devotional works, no religious music, and an education brutally atheistic and secular. In those days the old anti-God museums were flourishing (which were always, incidentally, a favourite haunt of visiting clergymen. I don't know quite why). All that was in full swing. So how could he arrive at this very understanding and sympathetic attitude to Christianity and to our Lord?

He made a remark which is one of the most extraordinary remarks anyone has ever made to me and has echoed in my mind more often than I can say. He said to me this: that if in this world you are confronted with absolute power, power unmitigated, unrestrained, extending to every area of human life— if you are confronted with power in those terms, you are driven to realise that the only possible response to it is not some alternative power arrangement, more humane, more enlightened. The only possible response to absolute power is the absolute love which our Lord brought into the world. Now this is to me a most significant fact, and I can see, though we in the West have not experienced this absolute power, that it would be so, that there would be something futile and ridiculous even in the attempt to meet such tyranny with some alternative propaganda or ideology. As between Caesar at his most absolute and God at his most remote, there is only Christ. And that was what this man said.

This process is going on in the hearts and minds of many citizens of the Communist countries. Even the authorities are beginning to admit it. For instance, a government-conducted survey actually announced in Leningrad not very long ago that thirty per cent of the population of the U.S.S.R. were believers. Now that's a vague expression, "believers," but as an admission from a government which had dedicated itself totally to destroying not just Christian faith, but every sort of transcendental belief, every tiny flicker of a transcendental idea—after sixty years of that in operation, it was an extraordinary admission.

Recently, we were making a television programme about the anti-God movement in the Communist countries and were filming a selection of their propaganda posters. The early ones all showed old peasants, old has-been people. But the latest posters showed young people as the ones being foolishly deluded by religion. So contrary to what might be expected, this fantastic steamroller trying to destroy every trace of Christian faith has failed. All the efforts of the most powerful government that's ever existed in the world, in the sense of taking to itself

the most power over its citizenry, have been unable
to shape these people into the sort of citizens it wants
them to be. Of all the signs of our times, this is the
one that should rejoice the heart of any Christian
most, and for that matter of anyone who loves the
true creativity of our mortal existence.

The best example of the incarnate presence of
Christ to withstand worldly power is Solzhenitsyn,
the most distinguished contemporary Russian writer.
It's a strange thing. I was making a programme on
Tolstoy in Russia when the Solzhenitsyn row broke,
and there was absolutely nothing about it in the Soviet
press. But we were filming at a house in Moscow
which is the house that Tolstoy had in *War and Peace*
as the residence of the Rostov family. In front of this
house is a huge statue of Tolstoy. It is now the head-
quarters of the Writers' Union, the organization which
enforces orthodoxy upon all Soviet writers. As we
filmed and as I held forth by the statue about Tolstoy,
people were coming in and out, signing a resolution
that Solzhenitsyn should be expelled from the Union
of Writers. This would mean he could no longer pub-
lish. It gave me a curious feeling to see these rather
sheepish figures coming and going, signing the peti-
tion, while I was holding forth under the shadow of
this vast statue of Tolstoy. Anyway, Solzhenitsyn was
sent into compulsory exile. If he had wished, he
could have remained in the U.S.S.R. as the most
successful, the most favoured, the most indulged
writer. His work *A Day in the Life of Ivan Denisovich*

had been published. He had been acclaimed in all the literary journals, and by being a little careful he could perfectly well have remained there and continued to write, enjoying fame and travel abroad. The reason he didn't choose this was that in his prison camp he had learned something he hadn't known before. He had learned in the prison camp the one thing you would have expected him not to learn, what it really means to be free. He realized that we can be free only if we are free in our souls; that a man in a prison camp who has learned to be free inside himself is freer than the freest man, whether in the so-called free world of the West or in the ideological Marxist world of the East. That is what he has expounded with such brilliance in his writing ever since.

One chapter in his second Gulag book is called "The Ascent." In that chapter he describes this process of illumination in a classic document of what it means to be liberated, to be free through Christ. St. Paul called it "the glorious freedom of the children of God,"[3] the only authentic freedom that exists in this mortal life. In one passage Solzhenitsyn says this:

> It was in my prison camp that for the first time I understood reality. It was there that I realized that the line between good and evil passes not between countries, not between political parties, not between classes, but down, straight down each separate individual human heart.

[3]Romans 8:21.

Then he adds, "It was on rotting straw in my labour camp that I learned this and I thank you, prison, for teaching me this truth."[4] So wonderful is the revelation Solzhenitsyn achieved in his prison life that his gratitude comes not for being freed from prison but for being sent into this prison camp.

Another episode described in one of his books is lodged firmly in my memory. He describes how in the bunk above his, in that terrible place, there was a man who in some extraordinary way remained serene, cheerful, brotherly. Solzhenitsyn observed that in the evenings, when this man lay down in his bunk, he would pull out of his pocket pieces of paper on which things were scribbled. He discovered that these were words copied from the Bible, from the Gospels.[5] That was another tremendous illumination to him. But these words scribbled out on a piece of paper and pulled out to look at in such grisly circumstances transformed this man from a broken, sour, bitter prisoner, into a brotherly, loving, fellow human being. I suggest that this is a miracle of our time.

Anatoli Kusnyetsov, the Soviet writer whom I in-

[4]Alexander Solzhenitsyn, *The Gulag Archipelago, 1918-1956; An Experiment in Literary Investigation* (New York: Harper & Row, 1973-), translated by Thomas P. Whitney. Volume II (1975), p. 615.

[5]Alexander Solzhenitsyn, *A Day in the Life of Ivan Denisovich* (New York: Dutton, 1963), translated by Ralph Parker. In the opening pages of the volume Ivan Denisovich Shukhov observes Alyosha the Baptist reading the New Testament.

terviewed, said, when asked how it was that he had this Christian orientation, that Stalin made one fatal error: he neglected to suppress the works of Tolstoy. Again I detect a miracle. If you scoured the literature of the centuries of Christendom for the books that might most help an oppressed people in relation to our Lord and the Christian faith, you could find nothing better than the short stories and the later novels of Tolstoy. The efforts of Radio Free Europe, Radio Liberation, the Voice of America, and the Overseas Service of the BBC, all put together, wouldn't equal one single short story of Tolstoy in keeping alive in the hearts of human beings the knowledge of the love of God. Tolstoy says so simply that we in this world, with all its difficulties and all the tumults of its history, have this marvellous possibility through the Incarnation of falling in with our Creator's purposes and rising above whatever circumstances there may be to trouble and hurt us—of rising into an awareness of that light which came into the world with the Incarnation, that great creative force that was released through the cross and through the resurrection.

Solzhenitsyn's address on the occasion of receiving a Nobel Prize is one of the great documents of our time. I love this passage:

> In agonizing moments in camps, in columns of prisoners at night, in the freezing darkness through which the lanterns shone, there often arose in our throats something we wanted to shout out to the

whole world, if only the world could have heard one of us. Such ideas come not from books and were not borrowed for the sake of harmony or coherence. They were formulated in prison cells and around forest campfires, in conversations with persons now dead, were hardened by that life developed out of there.[6]

To the great honour and glory of Solzhenitsyn, he was determined to speak of the camps and of his comrades there, so many of whom had died and been left behind. The cost has been that he has had to go into exile, that his life has been distorted, that he has been deprived of what to a writer is the most necessary thing, the environment of his native land and the possibility of writing in his native language, in order to be able to speak out on behalf of those people.

In the same address, he has some interesting words about the true task of an artist and a writer, words that we don't often hear nowadays in our part of the world:

The task of the artist is to sense more keenly than others the harmony of the world, the beauty and the outrage of what man has done to it, and poignantly, to let people know. Art warms even an icy and depressed heart, opening it to lofty, personal experience. By means of art we are some-

[6]Alexander Solzhenitsyn, 'One Word of Truth...': The Nobel Lecture on Literature (London: The Bodley Head, 1978), p. 8.

times sent dimly, briefly, revelations unattainable by reason, like that little mirror in the fairy tales. Look into it and you will see not yourself but for a moment, that which passes understanding, a realm to which no man can ride or fly and for which the soul begins to ache.

Solzhenitsyn is not prepared to say that our way of life in the West represents the alternative to the enslavement that has been established in his own country. For that reason he is severely criticized in the media here and what he says is often distorted or not made available. He did an interview in London with the BBC which had a strong impact but was not acceptable to the major networks in the United States and Canada. It contains one passage I found of particular interest. He says,

And it was only when I lay there on rotting prison straw that I sensed within myself the first stirrings of good. Gradually it was disclosed to me that the line separating good and evil passes not through states, nor between classes, nor between political parties either—but right through every human heart—and through all human hearts.... All the writers who wrote about prison but did not themselves serve time there considered it their duty to express sympathy for prisoners and to curse prison. I...have served enough time there. I nourished my soul there, and I say without hesitation: "*Bless you, prison,* for having been in my life."[7]

[7]Solzhenitsyn, *The Gulag Archipelago,* Volume II, p. 615.

Who would have believed in the days when I was there in Moscow that a distinguished Soviet citizen would one day write these words: "I myself see Christianity today as the only living spiritual force capable of undertaking the spiritual healing of Russia." Marxism he describes as a farce:

After all, this ideology has long ceased to be helpful. Nothing constructive rests upon it. It's a sham cardboard theatrical prop. For a long time now everything has rested solely on material calculation and the subjection of the people, not on any upsurge of ideological enthusiasm. The ideology does nothing now but sap our strength and bind us. It clogs up the whole life of society—minds, tongues, radio and press—with lies, lies, lies. This universal, obligatory forceable feeding with lies is now the most agonizing aspect of existence in our country, worse than all our material miseries, worse than any lack of civil liberties.[8]

We have been vouchsafed in the confusion and complexities of today an amazing sign that the promises Christianity enshrines are valid promises. Far from this faith's being, as the media here would have us believe, something that is over and done with, it represents on the contrary, in the desperate circumstances that Solzhenitsyn describes, the only possibility of being released, being liberated, being reborn.

Of course, it's all too easy to ridicule the absur-

[8]Solzhenitsyn, *The Gulag Archipelago,* Volume II, p. 617.

dities and contradictions of our present way of life, issuing denunciations in the mode of some twentieth-century Jeremiah. To do so is highly satisfying to the ego but should be resisted. Here I am speaking to myself.

Built into life is a strong vein of irony for which we should only be grateful to our Creator. It helps us to find our way through the fantasy that encompasses us to the reality of our existence. God has mercifully made the fantasies—the pursuit of power, of sensual satisfaction, of money, of learning, of celebrity, of happiness—so preposterously unrewarding that we are forced to turn to him for help and for mercy. We seek wealth and find we've accumulated worthless pieces of paper. We seek security and find we've acquired the means to blow ourselves and our little earth to smithereens. We seek carnal indulgence only to find ourselves involved in the prevailing erotomania. Looking for freedom, we infallibly fall into the servitude of self-gratification or, collectively, of a Gulag Archipelago.

We look back on history and what do we see? Empires rising and falling, revolutions and counter revolutions, wealth accumulating and wealth disbursed, one nation dominant and then another. Shakespeare speaks of "the rise and fall of great ones that ebb and flow with the moon."[9] In one lifetime I have seen my fellow countrymen ruling over a

[9]*King Lear,* V.ii.18-19.

quarter of the world, the great majority of them convinced, in the words of what is still a favourite song,
that "God who's made the mighty would make them
mightier yet." I've heard a crazed, cracked Austrian
proclaim to the world the establishment of a German
Reich that would last for a thousand years; an Italian
clown announce that he would restart the calendar
to begin with his own assumption of power; a mur-
derous Georgian brigand in the Kremlin acclaimed
by the intellectual elite of the Western world as wiser
than Solomon, more enlightened than Asoka, more
humane than Marcus Aurelius. I've seen America
wealthier and in terms of weaponry more powerful
than all the rest of the world put together, so that
Americans, had they so wished, could have outdone
an Alexander or a Julius Caesar in the range and
scale of their conquests. All in one little lifetime. All
gone with the wind. England now part of an island
off the coast of Europe and threatened with dismem-
berment and bankruptcy. Hitler and Mussolini dead
and remembered only in infamy. Stalin a forbidden
name in the regime he helped to found and domi-
nated for some three decades. America haunted by
fears of running out of the precious fluid that keeps
the motorways roaring and the smog settling, with
troubled memories of a disastrous campaign in Viet-
nam and of the great victory of the Don Quixotes of
the media when they charged the windmills of
Watergate.

Can this really be what life is about, as the media

insist? This interminable soap opera going on from century to century, from era to era, whose old discarded sets and props litter the earth? Surely not. Was it to provide a location for so repetitive and ribald a performance that the universe was created and man came into existence? I can't believe it. If this were all, then the cynics, the hedonists, and the suicides would be right. The most we can hope for from life is some passing amusement, some gratification of our senses, and death. But it's not all.

Thanks to the great mercy and marvel of the Incarnation, the cosmic scene is resolved into a human drama. God reaches down to relate himself to man, and man reaches up to relate himself to God. Time looks into eternity and eternity into time, making now always and always now. Everything is transformed by this sublime drama of the Incarnation, God's special parable for fallen man in a fallen world. The way opens before us that was charted in the birth, ministry, death, and resurrection of Jesus Christ, a way that successive generations of believers have striven to follow. They have derived therefrom the moral, spiritual, and intellectual creativity out of which has come everything truly great in our art, our literature, our music. From that source comes the splendour of the great cathedrals and the illumination of the saints and mystics, as well as countless lives of dedication, men and women serving their God and loving their Saviour in humility and faith.

If this Christian revelation is true, then it must be

true for all times and in all circumstances. Whatever may happen, however seemingly inimical to it may be the world's going and those who preside over the world's affairs, the truth of the Incarnation remains intact and inviolate. Christendom, like other civilizations before it, is subject to decay and must sometime decompose and disappear. The world's way of responding to intimations of decay is to engage equally in idiot hopes and idiot despair. On the one hand some new policy or discovery is confidently expected to put everything to rights: a new fuel, a new drug, détente, world government. On the other, some disaster is as confidently expected to prove our undoing. Capitalism will break down. Fuel will run out. Plutonium will lay us low. Atomic waste will kill us off. Overpopulation will suffocate us, or alternatively, a declining birth rate will put us more surely at the mercy of our enemies.

In Christian terms, such hopes and fears are equally beside the point. As Christians we know that here we have no continuing city, that crowns roll in the dust and every earthly kingdom must sometime flounder, whereas we acknowledge a king men did not crown and cannot dethrone, as we are citizens of a city of God they did not build and cannot destroy. Thus the apostle Paul wrote to the Christians in Rome, living in a society as depraved and dissolute as ours. Their games, like our television, specialized in spectacles of violence and eroticism. Paul exhorted them to be stedfast, unmovable, always abounding in God's work, to concern themselves with the things that are unseen, for the things which are seen are temporal but the things which are not seen are eternal.[10] It was in the breakdown of Rome that Christendom was born. Now in the breakdown of Christendom there are the same requirements and the same possibilities to eschew the fantasy of a disintegrating world and seek the reality of what is not seen and eternal, the reality of Christ.

I expect that you're all familiar with Plato's image of the shadows in a cave. The people in the cave saw shadows passing by and mistook these shadows, supposing that the shadows were people and that the names they gave them were real. I feel that this is an image of our existence. Our television is an outward and visible sign of this fantasy with which we preoccupy ourselves.

Many people here have asked me how it was that I came ultimately to be convinced that Christ was the answer. It was because in this world of fantasy in which my own occupation has particularly involved me, I have found in Christ the only true alternative. The shadow in the cave is like the media world of shadows. In contradistinction, Christ shows what life really is, and what our true destiny is. We escape from the cave. We emerge from the darkness and instead of shadows we have all around us the glory of God's creation. Instead of darkness we have light;

[10]1 Corinthians 15:58; 2 Corinthians 4:18.

instead of despair, hope; instead of time and the clocks ticking inexorably on, eternity, which never began and never ends and yet is sublimely now. What then is this reality of Christ, contrasting with all the fantasies whereby men seek to evade it, fantasies of the ego, of the appetites, of power or success, of the mind and the will, the reality valid when first lived and expounded by our Lord himself two thousand years ago? It has buoyed up Western man through all the vicissitudes and uncertainty of Christendom's centuries, and is available today when it's more needed, perhaps, than ever before, as it will be available tomorrow and forever. It is simply this: by identifying ourselves with Christ, by absorbing ourselves in his teaching, by living out the drama of his life with him, including especially the passion, that powerhouse of love and creativity—by living with, by, and in him, we can be reborn to become new men and women in a new world.

It sounds crazy, as it did to Nicodemus, an early intellectual and a potential BBC panelist who asked how in the world it was possible for someone already born to go back into the womb and be born again. It happens. It has happened innumerable times. It goes on happening. The testimony to this effect is overwhelming. Suddenly to be caught up in the wonder of God's love flooding the universe, made aware of the stupendous creativity which animates all life, of our own participation in it, every colour brighter, every meaning clearer, every shape more shapely, every note more musical, every word written and spoken more explicit. Above all, every human face, all human companionship, all human encounters, recognizably a family affair. The animals too, flying, prowling, burrowing, all their diverse cries and grunts and bellowings, and the majestic hilltops, the gaunt rocks giving their blessed shade, and the rivers faithfully making their way to the sea, all irradiated with this same glory for the eyes of the reborn. What other fulfillment is there, I ask, that could possibly compare with this? What going to the moon or exploration of the universe, what victory or defeat, what revolution or counterrevolution, what putting down of the mighty from their seats and exaltation of the humble and meek, who then of course become mighty in their turn and fit to be put down? This is a fulfillment that transcends all human fulfilling and yet is accessible to all humans, based on the absolutes of love rather than the relativities of justice, on the universality of brotherhood rather than the particularity of equality, on the perfect service which is freedom rather than the perfect servitude which purports to be freedom.

Nor need we despair to be living in a time when we have lost an empire on which the sun never set. It's in the breakdown of power that we may discern its true nature, and when power seems strong and firm that we're most liable to be taken in and suppose it can be used to enhance human freedom and well-being. We become forgetful that Jesus is the prophet of the losers' not the victors' camp, the one who proclaims that the first will be last, that the weak are the strong and the fools are the wise.

Let us then as Christians rejoice that we see around us on every hand the decay of the institutions and instruments of power, see intimations of empires falling to pieces, money in total disarray, dictators and parliamentarians alike nonplussed by the confusion and conflicts which encompass them. For it is precisely when every earthly hope has been explored and found wanting, when every possibility of help from earthly sources has been sought and is not forthcoming, when every recourse this world offers, moral as well as material, has been explored to no effect, when in the shivering cold the last faggot has been thrown on the fire and in the gathering darkness every glimmer of light has finally flickered out, it's then that Christ's hand reaches out sure and firm. Then Christ's words bring their inexpressible comfort, then his light shines brightest, abolishing the darkness forever. So, finding in everything only deception and nothingness, the soul is constrained to have recourse to God himself and to rest content with him.

I started this three days with you that I have found so enormously uplifting and pleasurable by talking about Pascal and by quoting from Pascal. Now I end by quoting from Pascal, who gives his name to these lectures. I've had the honour of delivering the first and I would like to say how earnestly and sincerely I hope that they will become a marvellous institution which year by year will fulfill the purpose of those who have instituted them. I read from Pascal's *Les Pensées*:

> What sort of monster then is man? What a novelty? What a portent? What a chaos? What a mass of contradictions? What a prodigy? Judge of all things. A ridiculous earthworm who is the repository of truth, a sink of uncertainty and error, the glory and the scum of the earth. Who shall unravel such a tangle? It is certainly beyond the powers of dogmatism and skepticism and all human philosophy. Man transcends man. Let us therefore grant to the skeptics what they've so often proclaimed, that truth is not within our reach, nor is it our prey, that it does not dwell on earth, that it's the familiar of heaven, that it lodges in the bosom of God and that it can only be known insofar as it pleases Him to reveal it. Let us learn about our true nature from uncreated and incarnate truth. Nature confounds the skeptics and reason confounds the dogmatists. What then will become of you, oh men, who seek to discover your true condition through your natural reason? You cannot avoid one of these sects or live with any of them. Know then, proud man, what a paradox you are to yourself. Humble yourself, impotent reason. Be silent, dullwitted nature and learn from your master your true condition, which you do not know. Listen to God.[11]

[11]Pascal, *Pensées*, 131.

QUESTION 1:

Mr. Muggeridge, I'd like to ask whether you feel Christ has any plans for his humanity in the church, or is it part of the Christendom which will terminate? I'm concerned with the church as a corporate, functioning body. You have shared with us some of the significant things the Lord has done in individual people, but my concern is with the church as a functioning body. Do you see that ending up on the scrap heap with the rest of Christendom?

MUGGERIDGE:

It entirely depends on whether the churches remain true to the Gospel of Christ, whether they truly expound his Gospel, whether they truly express his revelation. If they do, then clearly they won't die, even though in some aspects they might come to grief. It depends entirely on that. There's no other factor in the thing. They wouldn't succeed because they had great wealth or because they had great power or because they attracted very brilliant people. None of that would count, unless they are really and truly doing what our Lord said, ensuring that his light shine. If they do that, then their part is assured.

QUESTION 2:

If you were asked to do a Fourth Testament, whom would you choose as your subject?

MUGGERIDGE:

Two people that would interest me very much would

be Solzhenitsyn and John Henry Newman. Those are the two that I would choose.

QUESTION 3:

What are your views on evolution?

MUGGERIDGE:

I myself am convinced that the theory of evolution, especially the extent to which it's been applied, will be one of the great jokes in the history books in the future. Posterity will marvel that so very flimsy and dubious an hypothesis could be accepted with the incredible credulity that it has. I think I spoke to you before about this age as one of the most credulous in history, and I would include evolution as an example. I'm very happy to say I live near a place called Piltdown. I like to drive there because it gives me a special glow. You probably know that a skull was discovered there and no less than five hundred doctoral theses were written on the subject and then it was discovered that the skull was a practical joke by a worthy dentist in Hastings who'd hurriedly put a few bones together, not even from the same animal, and buried them and stirred up all this business. So I'm not a great man for bones.

QUESTION 4:

Mr. Muggeridge, next week Richard Leakey is going to be speaking here on evolution. My question is, supposing you are mistaken that the theory of evolution will be a curiosity. What effect does this have on Christianity, if any?

MUGGERIDGE:

I don't believe it's true.

QUESTIONER:

That's not the point.

MUGGERIDGE:

But it is the point. I beg your pardon. It's not your point but it's my point.

QUESTIONER:

I'm asking a hypothetical question. Would it make a difference to Christianity if evolution were true?

MUGGERIDGE:

Well, if it were true, I should have to consider that. But as it isn't true, I don't have to.

QUESTION 5:

Mr. Muggeridge, you say that it is a cause for rejoicing that the atheistic regimes have failed in sweeping Christ from their realms, but is it not equally a cause for rejoicing to the atheists that Christianity has failed in sweeping atheism from Christendom?

MUGGERIDGE:

I suppose so, yes. If I were an atheist I'd be rather well satisfied with the situation.

QUESTIONER:

How can you say that one is better or higher than the other?

MUGGERIDGE:

Only because I am a Christian.

QUESTION 6:

Mr. Muggeridge, I was interested in your comment toward the end of the presentation contrasting the absoluteness of love with the relativities of justice, and the universality of brotherhood with the particularity of equality. Would you care to clarify those distinctions? Many people think that love and justice are not differentiated along those lines.

MUGGERIDGE:

I hadn't thought of it as being obscure. The love that our Lord speaks of I would have said was an absolute. In other words, it applied to everyone. But the justice which is a human concept is particular in that it differentiates between one person and another. Similarly, brotherhood in the Christian sense is universal. All men and women are, from a Christian point of view, brothers and sisters, as being members of the same human family whose father is God. But the equality which is a political concept involves particularities, this person or that person. If I were a true Christian instead of a frail and hopeless old man, I would hope that I could love all men and women as, with me, children of God. But if you ask me to specify equality, then it is particular. I might be the equal of that person, inferior to that person, superior to that person. The political concept of equality in other words is particular. The Christian concept of love is universal.

QUESTION 7:

Mr. Muggeridge, what is the reality of Christ?

MUGGERIDGE:

I can answer you very shortly. The reality of Christ is Christ. Now that sounds like a trick, but it isn't. Whoever has known Christ, knows the reality of Christ. The reality of Christ lies in the fact that through him the distinction between fantasy and reality becomes clear. How can I find an image? I spoke earlier of the distinction that Blake makes between seeing with and seeing through the eye. Fantasy comes from seeing with the eye, from reflecting in your eye what is outside. Reality can be seen by looking through the eye. With Christ we look through rather than with.